To Way

from Granny & Poppo

2016

Pono Finds His Flippers

Story by Pattie McCann Tracy
with Illustrations by Chelsea Sachiko McKeown

For Jessica and Alisa, with love.

Pono Finds His Flippers

On an island far, far away, where the blue waters sparkle and the palm trees sway, lived a little boy named Pono.

The tropical sun kissed Pono's suntanned skin as he filled his days playing on the sandy shores with his best friend, a very happy Hawaiian monk seal named Lani.

They built sandcastles, collected seashells, and ate pineapples, mangos, kiwis and even a little SPAM.®
They had endless fun together.

Every afternoon, Lani swam in the sea where she played around and chased fish. Pono sadly watched as Lani had fun without him.

One night Pono's mom, Alora, asked, "Why are you so sad?"
"I don't have flippers like Lani, so I can't play in the sea."
Alora smiled saying, "Tomorrow I'll help you find your
flippers."

Excited, Pono fell fast asleep dreaming
of flippers all his own.

As the sun rose over the island the next morning, Pono
was already dressed in his swimming trunks when his
mom came into his room.

"Are you ready to find your flippers?"

"**Oh yes!**" Pono squealed with delight.

As they walked the sandy path to the water's edge, his mom said, "Pono darling, it's not about having flippers. Lani can play in the sea because she can swim."

"And today I'm going to teach you how to swim!"

His big brown eyes grew wide, and with surprise in his voice, he replied, "**Really**? I'll be able to swim with Lani?"

"Yes Pono my darling, you **will**."

15

Holding tightly onto his mother's hand, Pono stepped into the warm blue water.

With waves gently breaking at their feet, they looked up to see Lani swimming in the distance.

As Lani got closer, she popped her head up and shouted, "Aloha Pono, what's up brah?"

"I'm going to learn how to swim so I can play in the sea with you!"

Lani jumped for joy!

"The first fun thing we need to do is get the top of our heads wet," said Alora.

"Ready? One . . . two . . . three!"

"Make sure you blow bubbles."

With his mom and best friend by his side, Pono went underwater for the first time and blew bubbles.

20

"Don't worry, it only tickles for a second."

"Now let's keep going and make sure you can float on your tummy.

Keep your chin down and your eyes open."

"Good job! Are you ready to kick your feet?" Alora asked.

"Gently kick your feet and keep those legs straight."
With Lani close beside him, Pono kicked his feet and
glided through the warm, blue water.

"Kick, kick, kick," said his mom.

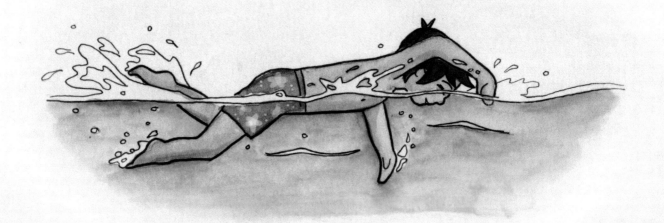

"Perfect. Now let's add your arms."

"How?" asked Pono.

"Just reach for the sun."

Pono tried really hard, reached high with
his arms and then put them softly back
into the water. "Way to go!" Alora and
Lani cheered.

And finally, after lots of practice,
Pono found his flippers . . .

and **learned to swim!**

"I'm hungry!"

"You did great Pono. Let's take a break and have some lunch," said his mom.

"You were amazing! You swam like a fish, only bigger and with arms and legs," Lani proudly told her best friend.

After lunch and a much-needed rest, Pono asked his mother if he could go back into the water.

"You can always go for a swim as long as you have an adult watching. Promise me you'll never go into the sea without an adult?"

"I promise, Mom."

Pono and Lani walked toward the sea. After a few steps, Pono stopped and ran back.

"Mahalo Mom – for helping me find my flippers. I love you."

He hugged her with all his might and lovingly kissed her face.

Pono and Lani ran across the sand and jumped in the water, splashing and playing. They floated on their backs, talking about their dreams and all the new adventures to come, giggling with glee.

The End.

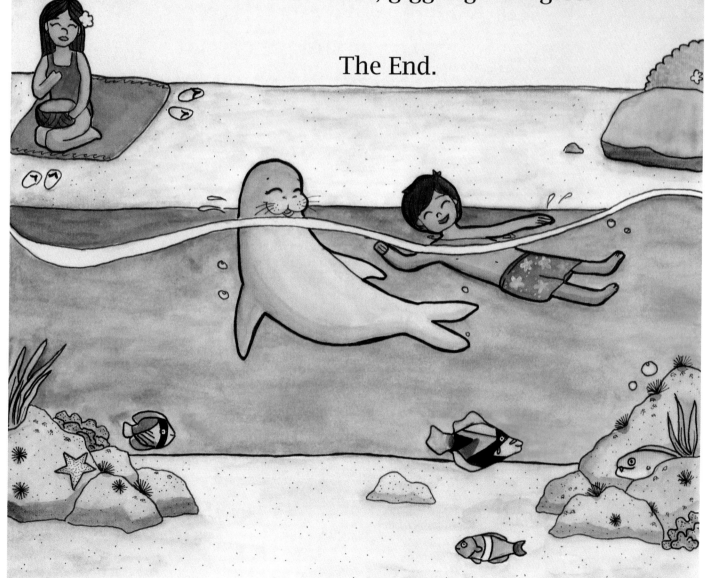

We hope you enjoyed
Pono and Lani's adventure.
Keep swimming and
reaching for the sun!

Story Guide*

Pono (PO-no) – "righteousness"

Lani (LA-nee) – "heaven" and, in some cases, "sky"

Alora (ah-LOR-ah) – "dream"

Aloha (ah-LO-ha) – "hello," "goodbye," "love," and "affection"

What's up brah? – "What's going on friend?"

Mahalo (ma-HA-lo) – "thank you"

SPAM® – a yummy canned meat product made mainly from ham that remains a versatile, high quality and great-tasting favorite in Hawaii.

*Derived from Hawaiian definitions/meaning

Draw a Picture of You and Your BFF.

Draw a Picture of You Swimming.

 Much Aloha.

55732132R00022

Made in the USA
Charleston, SC
02 May 2016